1·2·3 Draw
Wild Animals

A step by step guide

by Freddie Levin

Peel Productions, Inc.

Before you begin

You will need:

1. a pencil
2. an eraser
3. a pencil sharpener
4. lots of paper (recycle and re-use!)
5. colored pencils
6. a folder for saving work
7. a comfortable place to draw
8. good light

Now let's begin...!

Library of Congress Cataloging-in-Publication Data
Levin, Freddie.

  1-2-3 draw wild animals: a step by step guide / by Freddie Levin. p. cm.
  Includes index.
  ISBN 0-939217-42-2 (paper: alk. paper)
  1. Animals in art--Juvenile literature. 2. Wildlife art--Juvenile literature. 3. Drawing--Technique--Juvenile literature. [1. Animals in art. 2. Drawing--Technique.] I. Title: Wild animals. II. Title: One-two-three draw wild animals. III. Title.

NC780 .L44 2001 743.6--dc21   2001018530

Distributed to the trade and art markets in North America by

NORTH LIGHT BOOKS,
an imprint of F&W Publications, Inc.
4700 East Galbraith Road
Cincinnati, OH 45236

(800) 289-0963

Contents

Important drawing tip number 1:
*** Draw lightly at first, so you can erase extra lines. ***

Important drawing tip number 2:
*** Have fun drawing wild animals! ***

Important drawing tip number 3:
*** Practice, practice, practice and you **will** get better! ***

Circles, Ovals and Eggs

The drawings in this book start with three basic shapes:

 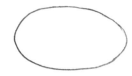 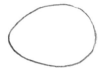

circle   **oval**   **egg**

*A circle is perfectly round.

*An oval is a squashed circle.

*An egg is an oval with one side fatter than the other.

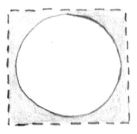 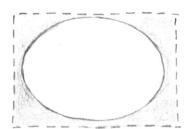 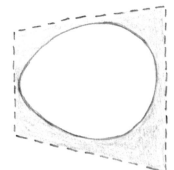

A **circle**
fits inside
a square.

An **oval**
fits inside
a rectangle.

An **egg**
fits inside
a trapezoid.

The more you practice drawing **circles, ovals** and **eggs,** the easier it will be.

Remember:

Draw lightly!

Note to parents and teachers:
I have found it helpful in working with very young children with poorly developed motor control to have them begin their drawings by tracing a small cardboard cutout of an egg, oval, or circle.

Bush baby

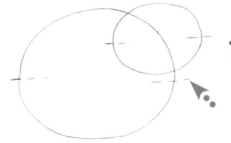

1 Start with a **circle** and an **oval**. Notice how they overlap.

2 Draw two ears, two big googly eyes, and a U shape for the nose.

3 Draw a long curling tail. Draw small **oval** toes.

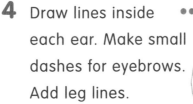

4 Draw lines inside each ear. Make small dashes for eyebrows. Add leg lines.

5 To finish the drawing, erase extra lines. Shade and color your bush baby. Give it a tree to sit in.

Bush babies are tiny tree-dwelling lemurs. They are nocturnal which means they are active at night. They are great leapers and their big googly eyes help them see in the dark. They eat insects, eggs, fruit and small animals.

Zebra

1 Start with a large **oval** and two **circles**: one small and one medium size. Notice the angles of the shapes and the distance between the three shapes.

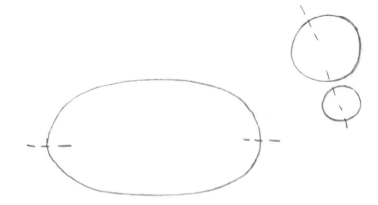

2 Connect the shapes with curved lines. Draw an ear and the beginning of a tail.

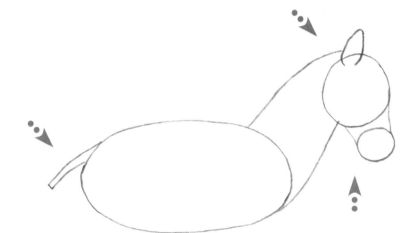

3 Draw an eye, nostril and mouth. Add the mane. Complete the tail. Draw the top sections of four legs.

4 Complete all four legs. Notice that each leg is in three sections.

5 To complete the drawing, erase extra lines. Add the zebra's spectacular stripes. They are complicated, so take your time and do a small section at a time.

Zebras are grazing animals that live in herds. A fancy cousin of the horse, each zebra's stripes are as individual as fingerprints. A mother zebra can tell which baby is hers by its stripes. Do you think it's like reading a bar code at the grocery store?

Elephant

1 Start with a **circle** and a big **oval**.

2 Add an eye. Draw a big ear. African elephants have bigger ears than their Asian cousins. Add a tail.

3 Draw the elephant's trunk and mouth. Add two sturdy legs. Finish the tail.

8

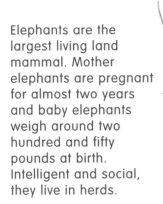

Elephants are the largest living land mammal. Mother elephants are pregnant for almost two years and baby elephants weigh around two hundred and fifty pounds at birth. Intelligent and social, they live in herds.

An elephant is the only animal with a trunk. Elephants use it to shower, carry food, cuddle a baby, sniff the wind, roll a heavy log, or greet a friend. When elephants meet each other, they put the tips of their trunks in each other's mouths.

4 Draw two more legs. Add a tusk.

5 To finish the drawing, erase extra lines. Add shading and color your elephant grey.

Excellent elephant!

Warthog

1 Start with a series of four **circles**. Draw the smallest lower than the others.

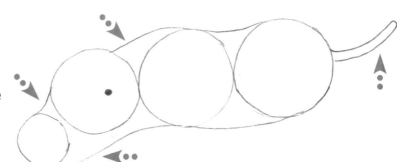

2 Carefully connect the **circles** with curved lines. Draw an eye and add the beginning of a tail.

3 Draw an **oval** with two small **circles** for the warthog's snout. Finish the tail. Draw two legs.

4 Draw ears. Add two more legs.

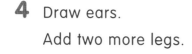

PRACTICE MAKES BETTER!

5 Add hooves and tusks. Draw lines inside the ears.

6 Draw a long bristly mane on the back and forehead.

7 To finish your drawing, erase extra lines. Shade your warthog and add color.

A warthog is a wild African pig. It lives in burrows, and likes to enter them backwards. Its tusks are used for digging and defense. The warthog diet consists of roots, eggs and small mammals.

Hippopotamus

1 Start with a big **oval** and two smaller **ovals**. Notice how the two small **ovals** overlap the bigger one.

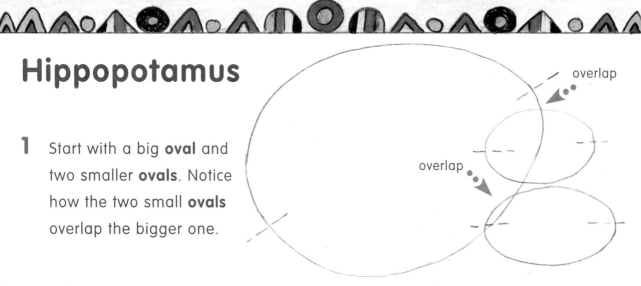

2 Connect the two smaller **ovals** with curved lines. Connect the head to the body with a curved line. Add two ears and eyes.

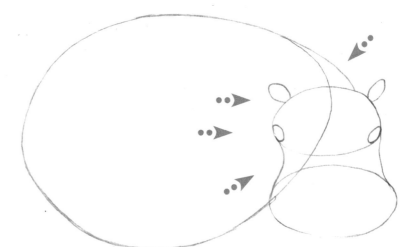

3 Draw nostrils. Add the lower jaw. Draw two legs.

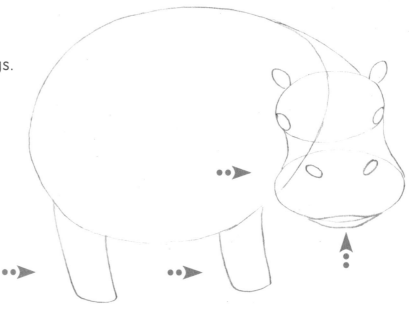

4 Draw another front and rear leg. Add a squiggly tale. Complete the face and ears.

5 Erase extra lines. Shade and color your hippo.

Happy Hippo!

The name 'hippopotamus' means 'river horse' but the hippo is more hog than horse. It lives near water and spends much of its time submerged with only its eyes, ears and nostrils showing. A hippo calf can swim immediately after birth and often nurses underwater. Hippos eat mainly fruit, leaves and grass...a lot of it!

Lion

1 Draw three **circles**.
Notice their positions.

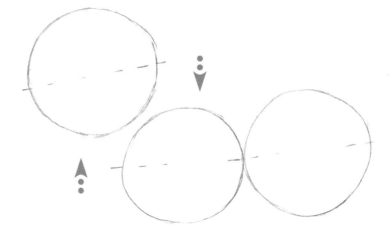

2 Use curved lines to
connect the neck and
body. Add ears, eyes and
a triangle nose.

3 Draw a mouth. Draw the
beginnings of the legs.
Add a tail.

4 Add the other rear leg. Draw the paws and finish the tail.

5 Erase the extra lines, shade and color. If it's a male lion, add a mane.

Adult male lions have a mane which grows in at around five to seven years old. Lions live in groups called prides. There is usually one male and several female lionesses plus the cubs. Lions eat mostly meat. The lionesses do most of the hunting and unless there are very young cubs, the male lion eats first.

Giraffe

1 Draw an **oval** and high above it, draw a smaller **oval**. (Can you guess why?)

2 Draw a small **circle** next to the small **oval**. Connect the head and body with two long neck lines. Draw a tail.

3 Draw curved lines to connect the circle and oval. Draw the mouth. Add an ear and a little horn. Start two legs.

4 Add another horn and lines inside the ear. Draw an eye and a nostril. Finish the tail. Draw more of the legs. Notice the round knee on the front leg.

5 Add a mane. Complete the legs. Add the hoof sections.

6 Erase extra lines, add shading and color. The square brown spots of a giraffe are a bit complicated, so do a little section at a time. They help the giraffe blend with the trees and protect it from sharp-eyed enemies.

Giraffes are the tallest land animals. Their long neck and legs lets them eat leaves from the tops of the trees. The word 'giraffe' comes from the Arabic word 'zarafa' which means 'charming'. They have big dark eyes, little knobby horns and an eighteen inch dark blue tongue.

Wildebeest

1 Draw a small **egg** and a large **egg**. Notice the direction of each **egg**.

2 Add an eye. Draw curved lines to connect the head and body, and to flatten the back.

3 Draw nostrils and a small indent at the cheek. Draw two legs.

4 Draw two more legs. Add ears. Draw a second eye.

Wild Animals from AFRICA

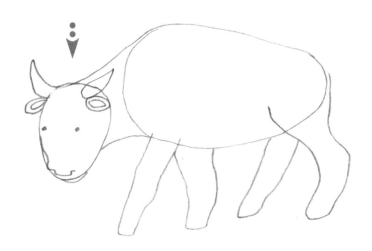

5 Draw two horns and the inside of the ear.

6 Add a tail. Draw a shaggy mane and beard.

7 Erase extra lines. Shade and color.

Wonderful wildebeest!

A wildebeest is a large African antelope. Wildebeests live in herds on the African grasslands called 'savannah'. Another name for wildebeest is 'gnu', pronounced NOO.

Panda

Pandas live in the bamboo forests that grow on upper mountain slopes in Southwest China and Tibet. They are extremely picky eaters—bamboo is the only food they eat!

1 Draw a vertical **egg** and put a **circle** on top of it.

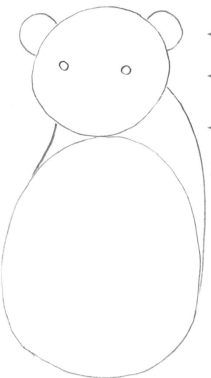

2 Connect the neck and back with curving lines. Add two ears and two eyes.

3 Draw the front leg and paw in three sections. Add a triangle nose and a small upside-down 'T' for the mouth. Draw a **circle** to begin the hind leg.

4 Draw **circles** around the eyes and **half-circles** in the ears. Add curves where the other front paw and second hind leg will be.

5 Draw two back paws.

6 To finish the panda, erase extra lines and color. Give your panda some bamboo to eat.

The panda is an adorable looking animal that resembles a stuffed toy. The adults are almost six feet tall and the babies are a tiny five ounces. Pandas are not really bears but in a class all their own.

Tiger

1 Draw a **circle** for the head and an an **egg** for the body.

2 Connect the **circle** and the **egg** with two curving neck lines. Draw two round ears, two eyes and a triangle nose.

3 Draw the inside of the ears. Add the mouth. Draw two legs.

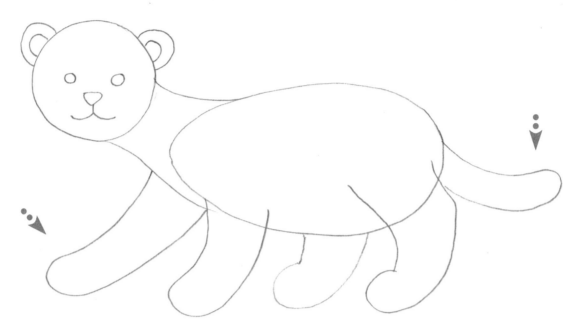

Tigers are the largest of the big cats. Unlike the sociable lion, tigers like to live alone. They hunt at night using their keen eyesight and although they don't climb very much, they are good swimmers. They are very adaptable and can live in many different climates from desert to swamp land.

4 Draw another front leg, another rear leg, and a tail.

5 Erase extra lines, shade and color. The tiger's beautiful stripes are complicated. Draw them a little at a time.

Terrific Tiger!

Orangutan

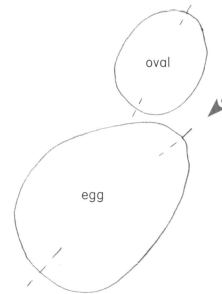

1 Draw an **oval** and an **egg**. Notice the angles of each.

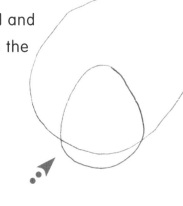

2 Add a small **oval** inside the **oval** and a small **egg** to the large **egg**.

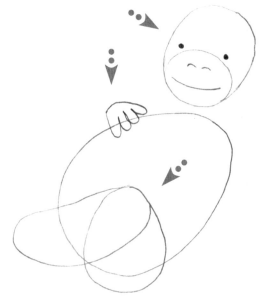

3 Draw the face: two eyes, two nostrils and a smiling mouth. Draw one hand. Now draw the lower leg.

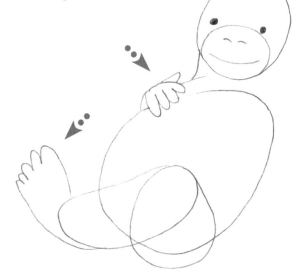

4 Add a curved neck line, the thumb and hand. Draw a foot.

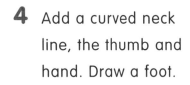

HAVE FUN!

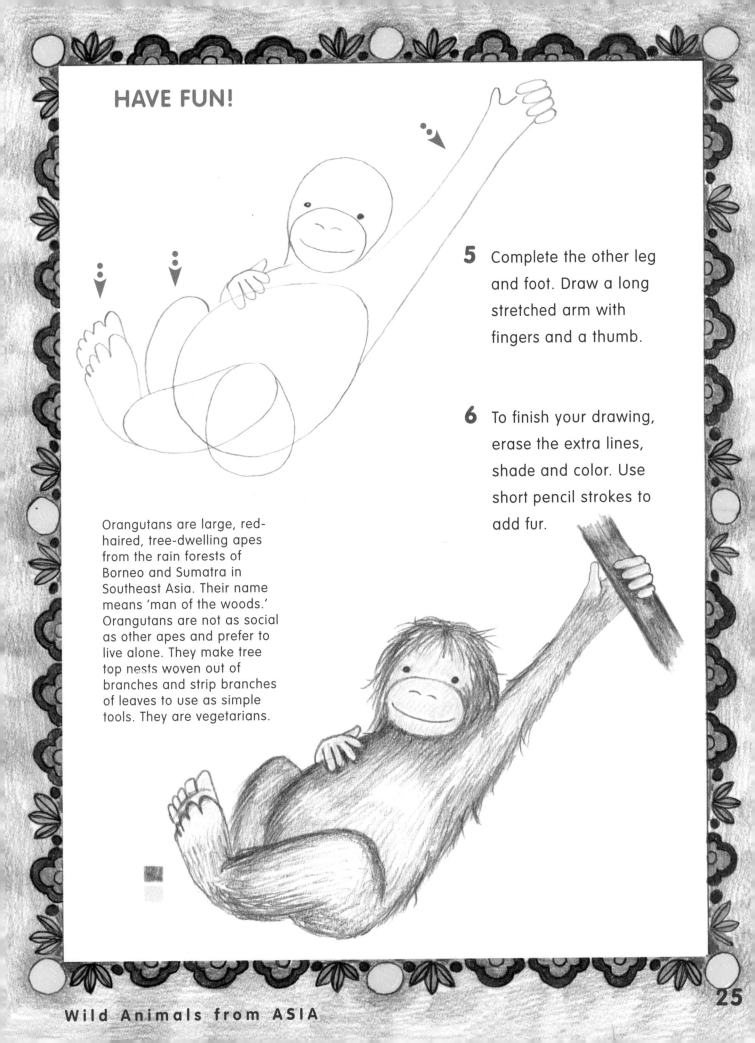

5 Complete the other leg and foot. Draw a long stretched arm with fingers and a thumb.

6 To finish your drawing, erase the extra lines, shade and color. Use short pencil strokes to add fur.

Orangutans are large, red-haired, tree-dwelling apes from the rain forests of Borneo and Sumatra in Southeast Asia. Their name means 'man of the woods.' Orangutans are not as social as other apes and prefer to live alone. They make tree top nests woven out of branches and strip branches of leaves to use as simple tools. They are vegetarians.

Rhinoceros

Rhinos are relatively peaceful but can be very fierce when it comes to defending their babies. A baby rhinoceros is pink when it is born. Rhinos like to be near water and they like a good mud bath. They are relatives of horses and are vegetarians. A rhinoceros looks clumsy but it can run surprisingly fast.

1 Draw a small **egg** and a larger **oval**.

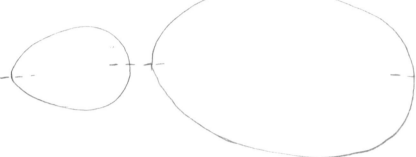

2 Add lines to form the head. Add an ear.

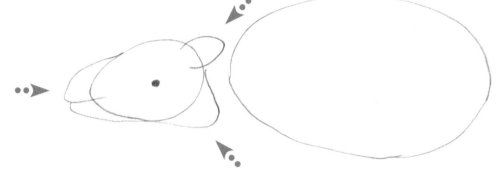

3 Draw lines to shape the shoulders and rump.

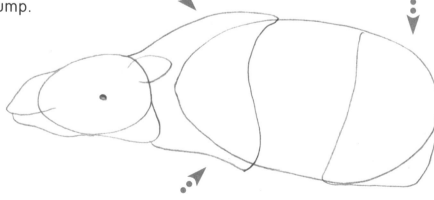

Wild Animals from ASIA

4 Draw another ear and a horn. Draw two sturdy legs. Begin the tail.

5 Add the nostril. Draw two more legs. Add toe nails. Finish the tail.

6 Erase extra lines. Shade and color.

Yak

1 Draw an **oval** and a small **egg**. Notice the angles of the shapes.

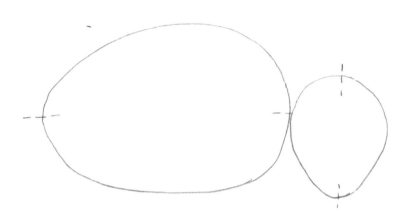

2 Draw lines to form the back and neck. Add an eye.

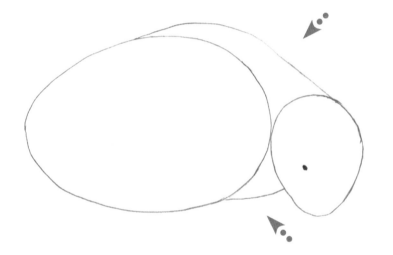

3 Add a line to shape the face. Draw two curving horns. Draw two legs.

The yak is the wild ox of Asia. It is larger than its domestic cousins.

28

4 Draw two more legs. Add a line for the nostrils.

5 Draw hooves. Add another eye.

6 Erase extra lines. Use long, light pencil strokes to make the yak shaggy. Finish coloring.

Yaks have thick woolly coats that can withstand the harsh mountain winds of the Himalayas. They are surprisingly agile and sure-footed on treacherous rocky paths. Yaks are almost six feet tall at the shoulder but carry their heads low, almost to the ground.

Armadillo

1 Draw an **oval** and a small **egg**. Notice the overlap and the angles of the shapes.

2 Add a line to shape the face. Draw a line for the neck. Add an eye.

3 Draw two ears. Draw lines to shape the bottom of the armadillo's body. Add two feet and a tail.

4 Draw the inside of the ear and the mouth. Add another leg. Draw curved lines on the back.

5 Erase extra lines. Shade and color the armadillo. Notice the markings and pattern of its 'armor.'

Insect-eating armadillos are nocturnal mammals that live in burrows in South and Central America and in some parts of the United States. Their leathery skin protects them. Some can also roll into a ball as a defense. Their funny, stiff gait makes them look a little like wind-up toys when they run.

Jaguar

1 Draw a **circle** and an **egg**.

2 Add a curved line for the neck. Draw two ears. Draw two eyes and a triangle nose. Add a tail.

3 Draw the front legs. Draw lines in the ears. Draw a line for the mouth. Add a curved line for the top of the back leg. Add the lower back leg.

4 Erase extra lines, shade and color. Carefully fill in the jaguar's beautiful spots. Notice that they are not round like polka dots, but have an irregular shape.

The jaguar is the biggest member of the cat family in the Western Hemisphere. A jaguar is an agile climber and a night hunter. It will eat any kind of meat.

Tapir **and her baby**

Shy, forest dwelling tapirs resemble large pigs but they are more closely related to horses and rhinos. They like to live near water and are excellent swimmers. Tapirs eat roots, leaves, twigs and fruit. The babies are born with spots that disappear as they mature.

1 Draw a small **circle** and a large **oval**. (Do the same for the baby, only smaller.)

2 Draw curved neck lines, and a bulge for the snout (nose). Add a small tail.

3 Add lines to form the lower jaw. Add an eye, two ears, and two legs.

DRAW LIGHTLY!

4 Draw two more legs.

5 Draw the inside of the ears. Add toes. Draw lines to shape the snout of the mother tapir. Give the baby stripes.

6 To complete your tapirs, erase extra lines, shade and color.

Sloth

1 Draw an **oval** and an **egg**. Notice the angles.

2 Draw a neck line. Add two long limbs.

3 Draw two more legs. Draw the features of the face.

Wild Animals from SOUTH AMERICA

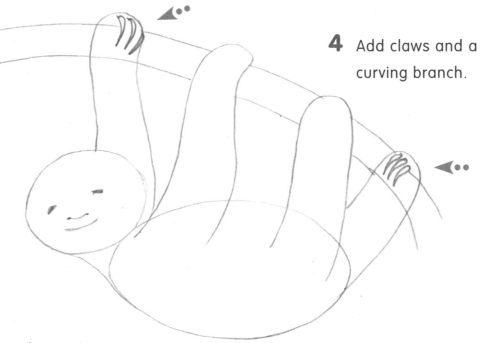

4 Add claws and a curving branch.

The sleepy, slow moving sloth spends most of its time hanging upside down from tree branches. It rarely comes down, finding all of the twigs, leaves and moisture it needs high up above the ground. It even sleeps that way.

5 Erase extra lines, shade and color. To make him shaggy, use short light pencil strokes.

Super sloth!

Guanaco

1 Draw a small **oval** and a larger **egg**.

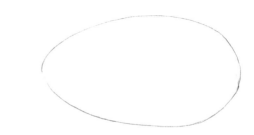

2 Add lines to form the face. Add a nostril, eye and ear. Draw curving neck lines.

3 Add another ear. Draw the tail. Draw two legs. Notice how the legs are divided into sections.

4 Draw two more legs. Add lines to the ears.

5 To complete the guanaco, erase extra lines, shade and color. Short light pencil strokes will make it look woolly.

Great Guanaco!

The guanaco is the wild cousin of the domesticated llama. Llamas, vicuñas, alpacas and guanacos are in the camel family. Guanacos live in the plains and mountains of South America. Its woolly coat is reddish brown and white. A baby guanaco is called a 'chulengo'.

Anteater

1 Draw a big **oval** and a
small **oval**. Notice the
angle of the small **oval**.

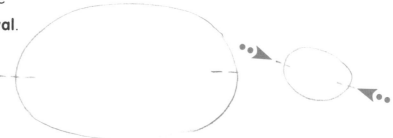

2 Draw curving neck lines
and a l-o-o-o-ng nose.
Add an eye and an ear.

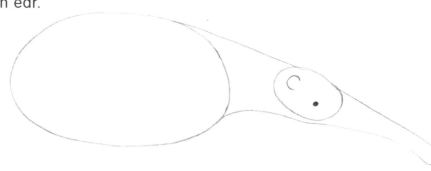

3 Draw the other ear and a
nostril. Draw three legs.

4 Make a tail. Use short pencil strokes to make it hairy. Add the fourth leg and draw l-o-o-ong claws.

5 Erase extra lines, shade and color. Note the markings on the anteater's side. Draw some ants for your anteater.

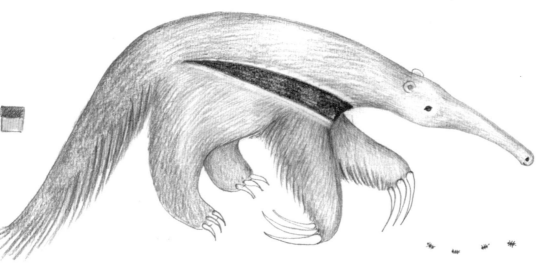

The anteater has nine inch claws and a long tube shaped head. It is perfectly adapted for ripping open nests and scooping up ants and termites with its tongue. The anteater is almost six feet long but its mouth is only one inch wide. It lives in the tropical forests and grassy plains of South America.

Peccary

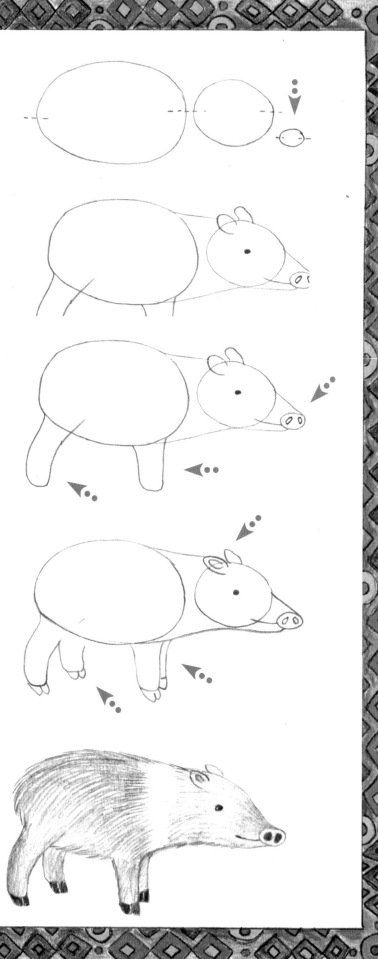

1 Draw a large **oval**, a smaller **oval** and a really small **oval**. Notice the position of the three **ovals**.

2 Draw lines for the neck, and two ears. Add an eye.

3 Draw lines to form the face. The smallest **oval** becomes the snout. Add two nostrils. Draw a mouth. Add two legs.

4 Draw two more legs and add hooves. Draw lines inside the ear.

5 Erase extra lines, shade and color. To make the bristly fur, use short, light pencil strokes.

The peccary is a wild pig. It lives mostly on roots and berries. It is shy and timid unless attacked. Another name for a peccary is a ' javeline.'

Skunk

1 Draw an **egg** and an **oval**.

2 Draw curved lines for the neck. Add the pointed nose. Draw an eye and an ear.

3 Add two legs and feet.

4 Draw two more legs and feet. Draw a tail. Add lines for the skunk's white stripe.

5 Erase extra lines, shade and color.

Super skunk!

The skunk is famous for its bad smell which it releases when frightened by an attacker. The odor is so powerful, it can be smelled almost a mile away and lasts for days. Skunks are in the weasel family. They eat insects, fruit and small animals. Skunk babies are called kittens.

Raccoon

1 Draw a large **egg** overlapping a smaller **egg**. Notice the angle of both.

overlap

2 Add two ears, two eyes, and a nose.

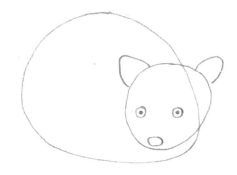

3 Draw front legs and paws.

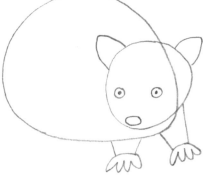

4 Draw a back leg and a big tail.

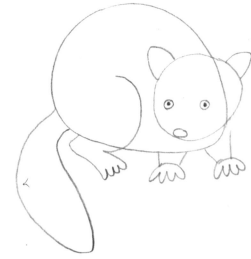

Wild Animals from NORTH AMERICA

5 Draw the face markings. Draw the inside of the ears. Draw stripes on the tail. Add a line to shape the stomach.

6 Add lines around the eyes.

7 To complete the raccoon, erase extra lines, shade and draw.

Raccoons have striped tails and black masks that make them look like little bandits. They are comfortable on the ground and in trees and prefer to make their homes in dens. They have skillful little paws that they can use almost like hands. Raccoons that live near people can be pests because they like to look for dinner in your garbage can.

Bighorn Sheep

DRAW LIGHTLY!

1 Draw a big **egg** and a small **egg**. Notice the angles.

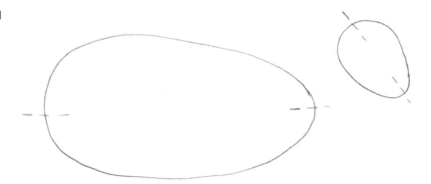

2 Add lines to form the face. Draw an eye. Add curving lines for the neck.

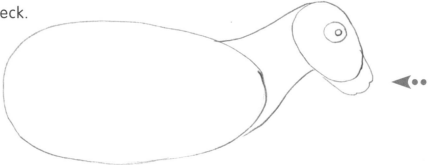

3 Draw the markings around the nose. Add two legs. Draw the tail and markings around it.

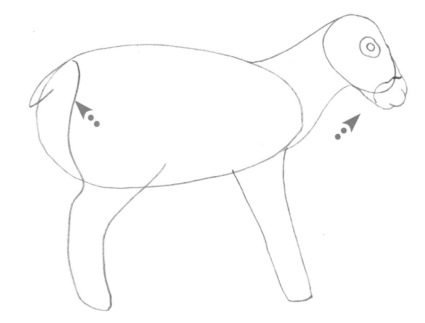

Wild Animals from NORTH AMERICA

4 Draw a big curling horn. Add two more legs.

5 Erase extra lines, shade and color the bighorn sheep.

Bighorn sheep live in the mountains of North America and on the Great Plains. The male has huge spiraling horns that give it its name. Bighorn sheep eat a variety of plants and grasses.

Prairie dog

1 Draw a skinny, vertical **egg**. Above it draw a small **egg**. Notice the angle.

2 Draw lines to form the nose. Add an eye. Draw curving neck lines.

3 Draw an ear. Add a front paw and a back leg.

4 Draw another back leg. Add a curving line to shape the stomach.

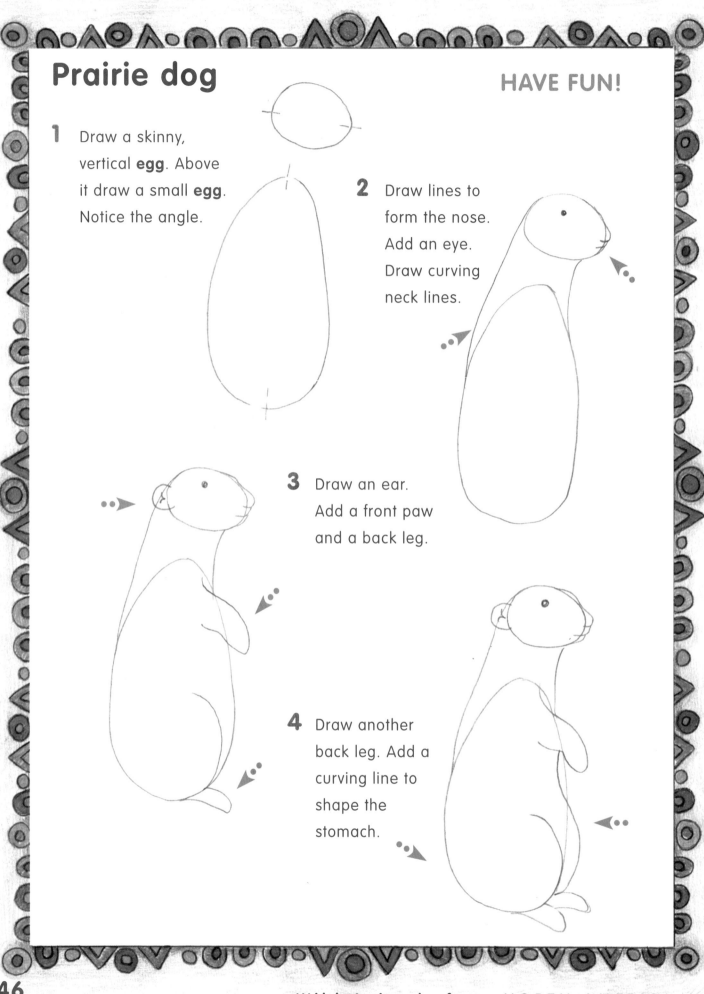

Wild Animals from NORTH AMERICA

5 Add a second front paw. Draw a tail.

6 Erase extra lines, shade and color. Make your prairie dog guarding the entrance to a burrow.

Prairie dogs are not dogs. They are relatives of squirrels. The name comes from its short, sharp bark. Prairie dogs are highly social animals and live in a community of connecting tunnels and burrows that is called a 'city'.

Bison (buffalo)

1 Draw a large **egg** and a small **egg**. Notice the position of both shapes.

2 Draw a curved line for the back of the neck. Draw an eye. Add two legs.

3 Add two horns. Draw the shaggy clump of hair on the bison's forehead. Add an ear. Draw the nose. Draw two more legs.

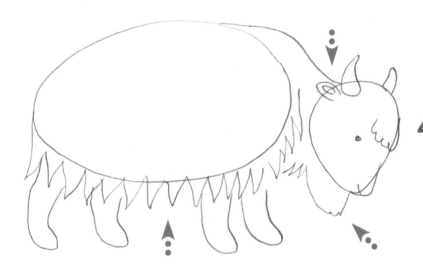

4 Draw the bison's shaggy fur. Make his shaggy beard. Draw the inside of the ear.

5 To complete your bison, erase extra lines, shade and color.

Beautiful bison!

The American bison is also commonly called a buffalo. Huge herds once roamed the plains from the Appalachian mountains to the western Rockies. They were an important part of the Native American way of life as a source of food, clothing and hides for shelters. In the 1800's, they were hunted almost to extinction, but with careful conservation, their numbers have increased.

Wolf

1 Draw a large **egg** and a small **egg**. Notice the position of the **eggs**.

2 Draw curved lines for the neck. Draw the nose and mouth.

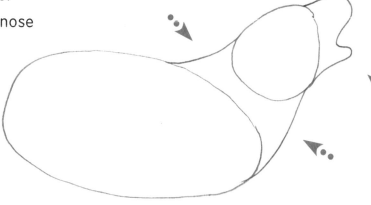

3 Draw the tip of the nose. Add an ear and eye. Draw two legs.

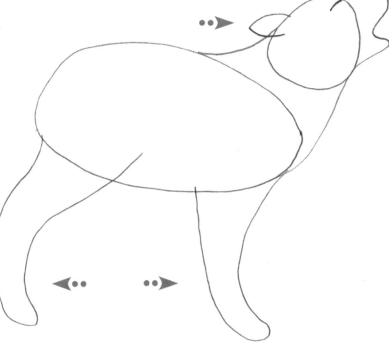

4 Add lines inside the ear and in the mouth. Add two more legs. Draw a tail.

A wolf is the largest member of the dog family. Wolves live in families called 'packs'. There are strong bonds of affection between the members of a wolf pack. They hunt together and defend each other from danger. The eery howl of a wolf pack is a beautiful and unforgettable sound.

5 Erase extra lines, shade and color. Use light pencil strokes to show the fur. Make a moon for your wolf to howl at.

Wonderful wolf!

Deer

1 Draw a large **egg** and a small **egg**.

2 Draw lines to form the face. Add an eye and an ear. Draw two curved lines to make the neck.

3 Draw the first antler. Add two legs.

DRAW LIGHTLY!

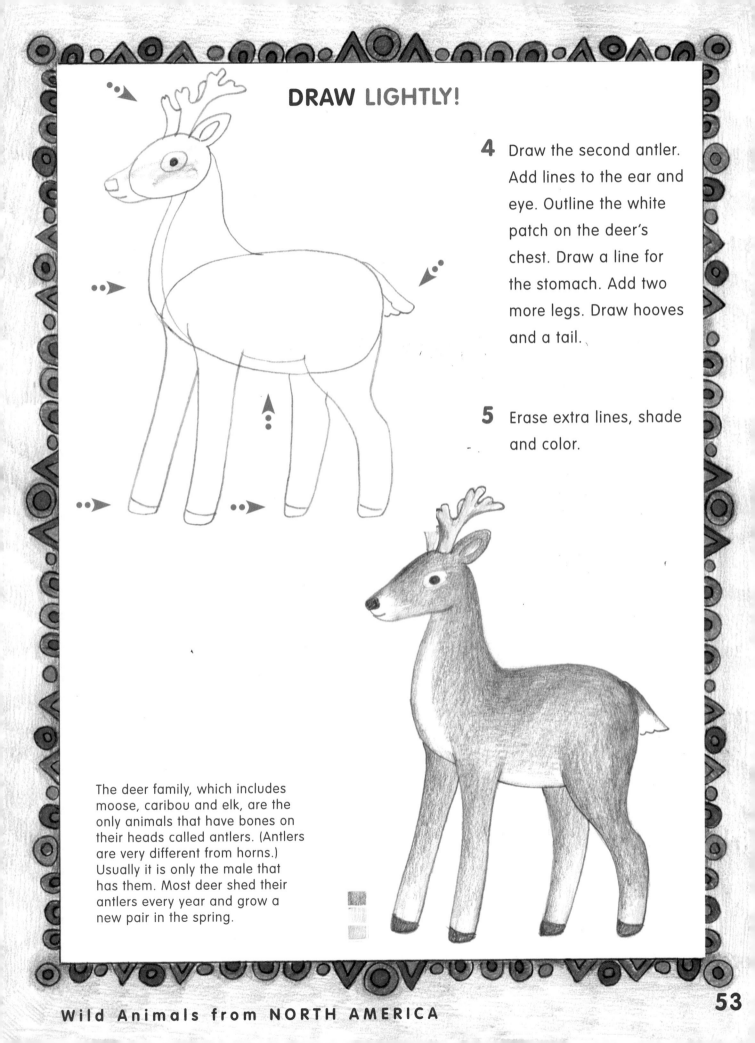

4 Draw the second antler. Add lines to the ear and eye. Outline the white patch on the deer's chest. Draw a line for the stomach. Add two more legs. Draw hooves and a tail.

5 Erase extra lines, shade and color.

The deer family, which includes moose, caribou and elk, are the only animals that have bones on their heads called antlers. (Antlers are very different from horns.) Usually it is only the male that has them. Most deer shed their antlers every year and grow a new pair in the spring.

Kangaroo

1 Draw a small **egg** and a large **egg**.

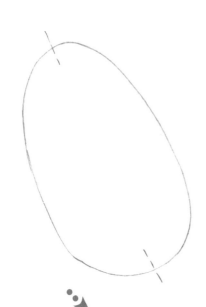

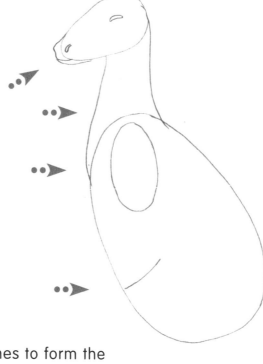

2 Draw lines to form the face. Add an eye and a nostril. Draw an **oval** for the upper arm. Make a line for the kangaroo's pouch.

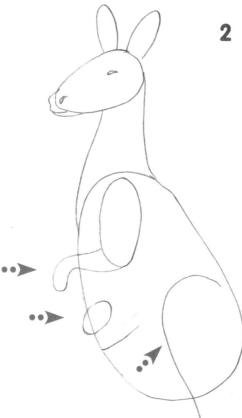

3 Draw two ears. Add the lower arm. Draw a tiny **oval** above the line of the pouch for the head of the kangaroo's joey. Add a curved line to start the hind leg.

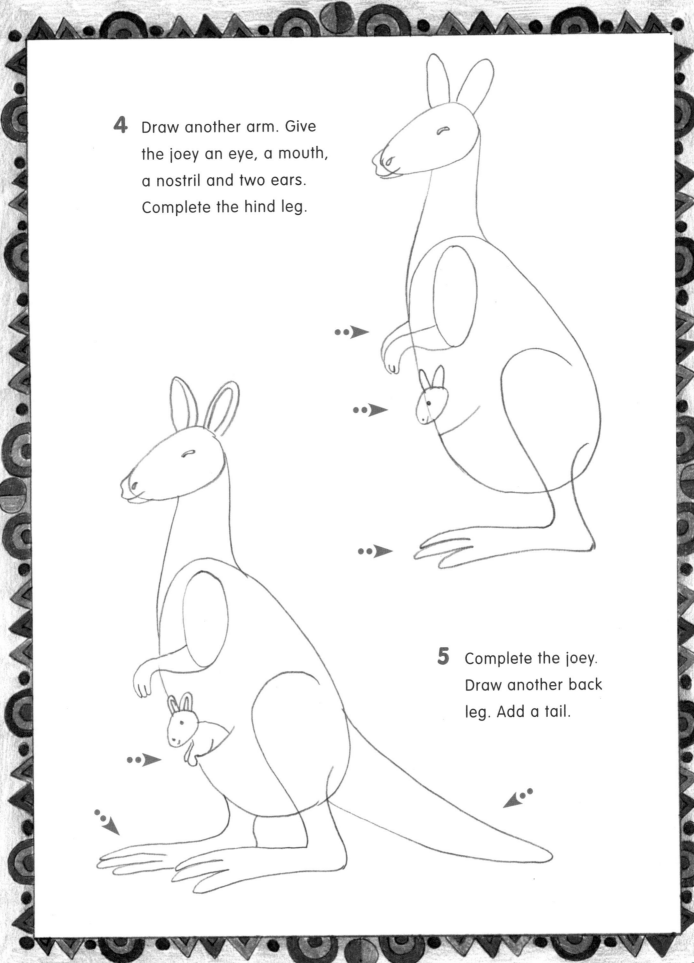

4 Draw another arm. Give the joey an eye, a mouth, a nostril and two ears. Complete the hind leg.

5 Complete the joey. Draw another back leg. Add a tail.

6 To complete your kangaroos, erase extra lines, shade and color.

Kangaroos are marsupials. This means that after their babies are born, they live in their mother's pouch until they are old enough to get around on their own. A baby kangaroo is called a 'joey'. Kangaroos are almost six feet tall. They eat grass and plants and travel in large groups called 'mobs'.

Platypus

1 Draw an **egg**. Notice the angle.

2 Add a tail and two legs. Draw two eyes. Add lines to begin the duck-like bill.

3 Draw the platypus' duck bill. Add another front leg.

4 Erase extra lines, shade and color.

Pretty Platypus!

The platypus is a mixed-up looking animal. It is one of only two egg-laying mammals (the other is the echidna). It has webbed feet and a snout that looks like a duck's bill. The platypus lives in burrows along Australian streams where it catches small shellfish, worms and grubs. It's about two feet long and only weighs about five pounds. Its fur makes it appear larger.

Wombat

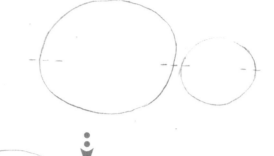

1 Draw a big **circle** and a smaller **circle**.

2 Draw two curved lines for the neck. Draw the face. Add an eye.

3 Draw two legs. Add an ear.

4 Draw a line inside the ear. Add another ear. Draw a nose. Draw two more legs.

5 Erase extra lines, shade and color.

Wonderful wombat!

A wombat is a short, stocky burrowing animal. It is nocturnal, which means it is active at night. It lives on grasses and roots. The wombat is a marsupial, and its pouch faces backwards, (the opposite of the kangaroo) so that as it digs, the flying dirt does not disturb its babies.

Koalas look like bears but they're not. These sleepy marsupials spend most of their lives in the fork of a eucalyptus tree, eating its leaves and shoots. They get all the moisture they need from the leaves. Their name, koala, is an Australian Aborigine word meaning 'no drink'.

Koala

1 Draw an **egg** and a **circle**. Notice how they overlap.

2 Draw two ears, two eyes and a triangle nose.

3 Add a triangle to the nose and a little upside down 'T'. Draw the front leg.

4 Draw lines inside the ears. Add two little eyebrows. Draw the back leg. Add claws.

5 Erase extra lines, shade and color. Put your koala in its favorite place: a eucalyptus (yoo-ka-LIP-tus) tree.

Cute koala!

Polar bear

1 Draw a big **oval** and a small **circle**.

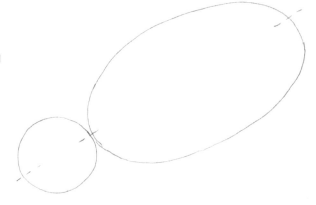

2 Draw the face. Add two ears and an eye. Add curved lines for the neck.

3 Draw two legs.

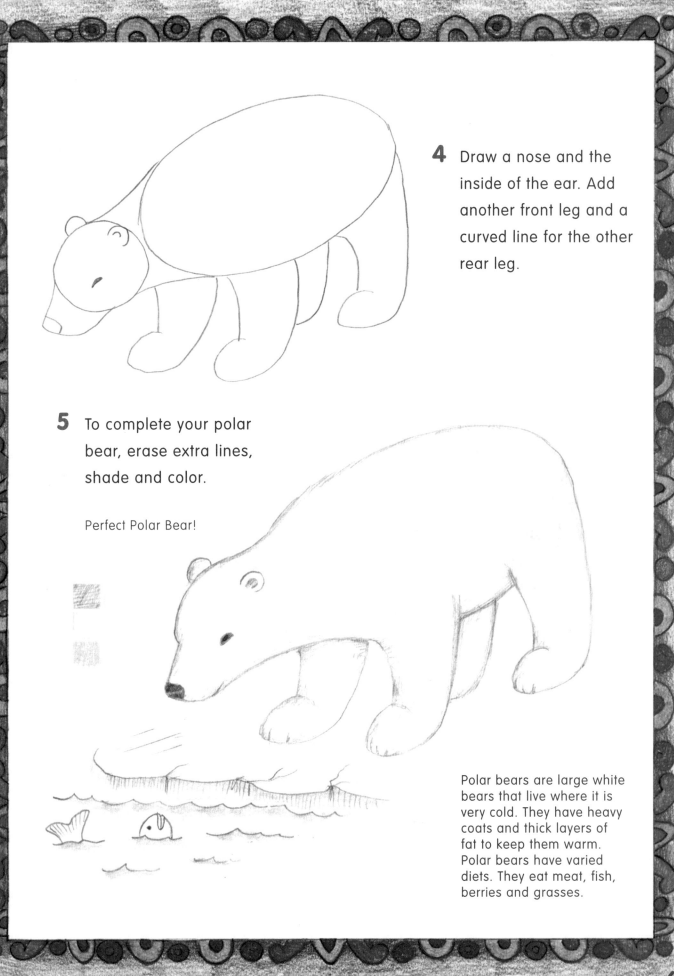

4 Draw a nose and the inside of the ear. Add another front leg and a curved line for the other rear leg.

5 To complete your polar bear, erase extra lines, shade and color.

Perfect Polar Bear!

Polar bears are large white bears that live where it is very cold. They have heavy coats and thick layers of fat to keep them warm. Polar bears have varied diets. They eat meat, fish, berries and grasses.

Walrus

1 Start with a big **egg** and a small **circle**.

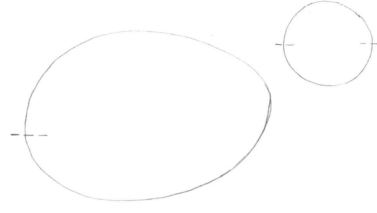

2 Draw a second **egg** around the small **circle**.

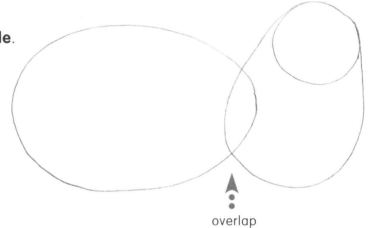

overlap

3 Add two curved lines for the neck and stomach. Add two eyes and a nose. Begin the rear flipper.

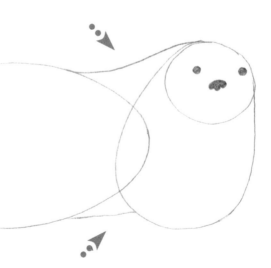

PRACTICE MAKES BETTER!

4 Finish the rear flipper. Draw lines for the muzzle underneath the walrus' nose.

5 Add two tusks. Draw two front flippers.

The walrus is a 'pinniped' which means that their feet, like a seal's, are flippers. Walruses are huge - up to fifteen feet long and over three thousand pounds. Their fat keeps them warm in the cold Arctic waters. They eat mostly clams and other shellfish. Walruses use their tusks as a weapon for defense, as a tool for digging up food and as a hook for climbing.

6 Erase extra lines, shade and color.

Index

Learn about other
drawing books online at
www.drawbooks.com!